Retired with Paid Hobbies:
How I Turned Freedom into Fun
By George Einhorn

RETIRED

WITH

PAID

HOBBIES

HOW I TURNED FUN INTO FREEDOM

George Einhorn

PURPOSE, PASSION, AND A PAYCHECK, A NEW RETIREMENT FORMULA

Nothing in this book is intended to serve as financial, legal, tax, medical, or retirement planning advice. Please consult qualified professionals before making decisions related to finances, health, or retirement.

Book design by Nate Myers
Cover design by Jose Fernandez Villamayor

ISBN (paperback)
ISBN (ebook)

First paperback edition April, 2026

Published by Second Act Press
Crete, Illinois 60417

For Julie...

YOU'VE BEEN THE STEADY HEARTBEAT behind every dream I've chased and every chapter I've written. In the everyday moments and the triumphant ones, you've been my warmth, laughter, calmness, and courage.

This book is about finding joy in what you love, and the greatest joy I've known is walking through life with you. My partner, my inspiration, my every day, this is for you. Thank you for believing in me when the page was blank, for cheering the loud and soft music, and for filling our life with a rhythm that feels like home.

Table of Contents

What Do You Do Now That You're Retired?

THIS BOOK GREW OUT OF a simple but persistent question people asked me when I retired: "So, what do you do now that you're retired?"

It's a legitimate question. Americans have been sold a limited picture of retirement: golfing, playing with grandkids, maybe going on a cruise. Retirement has a reputation: slow mornings, afternoon naps, and days that drift by. And while those types of things could very well be wonderful, if you've been a productive person your whole life, they're not going to cut it.

People love to ask me that question. It usually comes at the grocery store, a neighborhood party, or a local eatery, often from someone working full time and counting the days until they're free.

I smiled. "Well," I said, "I'm retired with paid hobbies."

Cue the double take.

But that's my reality. I teach part time at two local colleges, play the drums in a soul and R&B band, and get paid to do both. I don't get working wages but it's enough to make me feel like my time still has value.

I'd do these things even if no one paid me a dime. That's the point. After spending decades as a healthcare executive in the professional world of meetings, metrics, deadlines, and performance reviews, when I retired, I felt like I was stepping off the treadmill. The fun meter for my job had run out but I didn't want to sit still. I wanted to move, create, share, and stay connected with friends and colleagues.

Your answer to that question may not involve slowing down, either. You may be interested in rediscovering what you love to do, resurrecting abandoned talents, and exploring curiosities that may have been quietly waiting, sometimes hiding in plain sight, until you had more time.

Retirement doesn't have to mean ending the productive phase of your life. What if you could make it the most vibrant, creative, and rewarding phase, a time in which you could enjoy activities that align with your purpose and even earn a little income along the way?

You *can* make it about switching gears. You can begin the most fulfilling chapter of your life when your career ends, when you can finally spend time doing what you love, on your terms, with no boss, pressure, or Sunday-night dread.

You can redefine what it means to retire and turn your passions, skills, and curiosities into meaningful (and sometimes profitable) pursuits, whether that includes taking online art classes, mentoring young people, training for a seniors' triathlon, selling garage-sale finds online, or serving on your homeowner's association board.

Retired with Paid Hobbies features stories about real people and their experiences. If reading this book and these stories helps you imagine a second chapter you're excited about, and if you're encouraged to explore an activity because it brings you joy, then I've done what I set out to do.

In talking with retirees for this book, what surprised me most was how often retirement pursuits that people approached simply for joy, connection, or curiosity ended up generating a little income.

This book is about possibilities. It's about staying curious, staying engaged, and recognizing that when your career ends, you don't have to abandon the experiences you've had, skills you've built, or activities you love to do. It's about exploring what excites you in this season of your life, as well as finding ways to share your gifts with the world on your terms.

Whether you've just retired or you're imagining your post-career days down the road, the stories, principles, and steps in these pages will show you how to:

- Enliven your energy, creativity, and enthusiasm so they'll stay strong for the rest of your life
- Balance freedom, joy, and the ability to earn a little income
- Build meaningful connections with people

Retirement doesn't have to be your finish line; it can be your launchpad to an amazing next chapter of life. Instead of stopping, you can choose anew how you spend your time and what you decide is worth your energy.

Ready to flip the script and make your retirement about freedom, fun, and paid hobbies? Let's get started.

PART I:

Rethinking Retirement

CHAPTER 1

The Myth of the Golden Years

WHEN I WAS A KID, my parents' friends talked about the "golden years." It sounded like a magical time. The clouds would part, a brass band would play, and life would suddenly turn into one long, carefree vacation. You'd be finished with work, wake up whenever you wanted, play golf three times a week, maybe buy an RV, and drive off into a continual sunset.

That was the dream.

Fast-forward fifty years and I started wondering *whose* dream that was, exactly. Because when you actually get to retirement age, you realize something strange: It's not all golden. In fact, it can feel a little…anticlimactic.

Most people think of retirement as the ultimate prize at the end of a long, hard race. You grind for decades, pay your dues, raise your family, and tell yourself, "Just a few more years and I'll be free." We plan for it financially, obsessively, and endlessly: 401(k)s, Social Security, health benefits, savings targets. But what we don't plan for, and what no one really talks about, is *how we'll spend our time.*

The average retiree gains about 2,000 hours a year—the same amount of time most people spend working. That's 2,000 hours, that's 8 hours a day, 5 days a week for 50 weeks, staring you in the face. What are you going to *do* with all that time?

The first few months of your retirement, particularly if you've been working long hours on the job, might indeed feel like a vacation. Sleep in. Read. Catch up on Netflix. Take that long-awaited trip.

Then, around month six, you realize you can't golf every single day. You can't nap your way to fulfillment. Too much daytime TV and surfing social media will drain you of energy and make you question your faith in humanity.

That's when it hits: Retirement is not freedom *from something,* it's freedom *to do something else.*

A funny thing happens when you've got all the time in the world: you start missing the structure you used to complain about. The meetings, deadlines, colleagues (well, maybe not all of them). You miss the sense of purpose, the feeling that you mattered to someone, somewhere.

There's absolutely nothing wrong with slowing down. You've earned it. But slowing down isn't the same as stopping. In addition to worrying about running out of money, the real danger is running out of meaning.

In our parents' generation, people often had one career at one company, and the same expectation of retirement: stop working at 65 and start collecting your pension.

Times have certainly changed. Humans are living longer. The average life expectancy for men and women combined in the U.S is 78.4 years. We're healthier. We're better educated. We're wired for activity and curiosity. Many of us want to keep contributing, just without the bureaucracy, stress, or alarm clock set for 5 a.m. Now, retirement isn't about checking out, it's about tuning in. It's about asking yourself what you love enough to do for free, and hey, maybe could you do it in such a way that earns a little money?

Why leisure alone isn't enough

My true "golden years" started when I realized I didn't have to stop being productive; I just had to start playing. Teaching part time, performing with my band, mentoring students—those aren't jobs; they're extensions of who I am. The income reminds me that the world still values what I bring. "I'm retired with paid hobbies" is my philosophy because the real gold in these years isn't leisure, status, or rest. It's joy. It's purpose. It's waking up in the morning with something to look forward to that makes you smile, and maybe the chance to make someone else's day better.

CHAPTER 2

Not Finished, Just Getting Started

WHEN I TOLD PEOPLE I was retiring, the reactions were pretty consistent. "Congratulations! What are you going to do now?" And my favorite: "You're too young to retire!" I'd smile and say, "Don't worry. I'm not finished. I'm only 69. I'm just getting started."

Most people assumed that my response was a polite deflection. It wasn't.

For decades, we base our identities on our careers. We introduce ourselves by what we do:

"I'm a teacher."

"I'm a manager."

"I'm a homemaker."

"I'm a nurse."

"I'm an executive."

When that title goes away, you may feel like part of you goes with it. But here's the truth. Your job was never the whole story; it was just one component of your life. When you leave the full-time-work world, something interesting can happen. You realize you're still the

same person with the same skills, energy, drive, and personality traits…
only now, you're free to use them as you want.

No HR department. No performance reviews. No politics. No
kids living at home. Just pursuing your dreams on your terms.

Choice is a gift and a challenge

Reaching retirement gives you the gift of choice, something you
probably haven't had since you were a kid. For the first time in decades,
you get to decide:

- Which projects you do
- Where you put your energy
- Whom you spend time with

That's powerful. But choice can also be paralyzing. When every
door is open, which one do you walk through?

For me, when I stopped overthinking it, the answer was simple: go
back to what's always brought me joy—my north stars—the activities
that have made me feel most alive. Now I do them on my own schedule,
surrounded by people I want to be around.

That's the beauty of being retired with paid hobbies. You stop
chasing money and start attracting it.

In most jobs and careers, productivity is measured by output: how
much you produce, achieve, earn; how far you can get up the corporate
ladder. In retirement, the focus changes to input: what fills you up,
makes you happy, gives you a reason to get out of bed. I no longer
count hours or worry about deadlines. I count laughs, songs, classes,
and conversations that make me feel useful and alive. That's my new
metric for success. And here's the irony: when I stopped "working," I
started doing some of the best work of my life.

Some people think retirement means giving up your ambition. I
think it means redefining how you want to be ambitious. One musical

note, class, or human connection at a time, you can build a life that feels good. The secret most retirees never tell you is that the best years aren't necessarily behind you. They may be right in front of you, waiting to be shaped, played, painted, or taught into existence.

Now, when someone asks me how retirement's going, I tell them "I didn't retire to slow down. I retired to do more of what matters." And that's just the beginning.

CHAPTER 3

From Career to Calling

WHEN YOU STOP WORKING FULL time, the silence can be deafening. No more morning rush. No more meetings. No more inbox dinging like a slot machine.

At first, it's peaceful. Then it's a little eerie. You start wondering who you are without all that noise. If you're like many people, your career was the scaffolding that held up your sense of identity. Take away the title, the business card, the daily grind, and suddenly the question "What do you do?" gets more difficult to answer. But here's the twist. Retirement gives you the rare opportunity to rebuild your scaffolding around your calling.

A career is what you do for a living; what pays the bills and comes with obligations and expectations. Your callings are activities that fill your soul: things you'd still do even if nobody was watching or paying you to do them. For some people, a calling is hidden inside their career choice all along. For others, it's a passion they rediscover after decades. Maybe they discover their old drums in the basement, remember how much they enjoy mentoring, or resume making art after they gave it up for lack of time.

The key to this new chapter of your life isn't reinvention; it's rediscovery. You don't have to become someone new. You just have to remember who you were before the job title took over.

Ask yourself:

- What did I love doing before I was paid to do something?
- When do I lose track of time because I'm having so much fun?
- What gives me energy instead of making me feel tired?
- What have people always thanked or appreciated me for?

Your calling may be hiding in those answers.

For me, it was clear: I've always loved connecting with people through teaching, mentoring, and performing. The classroom and the stage are different arenas, but they share the same energy of engagement, rhythm, and connection.

Security vs. satisfaction

The traditional career model is built around security: steady income, benefits, your personal retirement plan. When your career ends, though, you need another kind of security: the comfort of knowing you're spending your time doing things that make you happy. No meetings that make your blood pressure rise. No pretending to care about initiatives you despise. When you find your calling, you don't need to fill your days with busyness; you can fill them with meaningful pursuits.

A calling doesn't necessarily mean starting a business, changing the world, or writing a bestseller. Sometimes the scope is smaller, like volunteering at an animal shelter or becoming a ham radio operator. The point isn't the scale; it's the spark. If it makes you feel alive, it counts.

Here's the best part. When you follow your callings, other people will feel it, too. Your joy becomes contagious. Students learn more when their teacher loves being there. Audiences connect more when songs come from musicians' hearts. Neighbors light up when they see someone living with purpose. That's the ripple effect of living your calling—it makes the world better. And if you happen to get paid along the way, that's the universe's way of telling you to keep doing it.

Think of your life as a song. Your career was the verse: structured, familiar, even repetitive. Your calling is the chorus—the part that lifts you up and that you want people to remember.

Are you ready to write your next verse? You're not finished. You're just hitting your groove.

CHAPTER 4

Why Too Much Idle Time Can Drive You Crazy

THERE'S A POPULAR FANTASY ABOUT retirement: you'll have all the time in the world, and you'll love every minute of it. No alarm clocks. No email. No traffic. Just long, lazy mornings with coffee and the crossword.

Many people find that for about two weeks, being retired feels like bliss. But then reality sets in. You start wondering, "What day is it?" With no work-week schedule, all the days run together. Every day feels like Saturday. You've done your "to-do list." And you're surprised to discover that too much free time doesn't feel freeing; it's like being in a fog.

We've been sold the idea that the ultimate reward for a lifetime of work is rest. Of course, rest is important. After forty-plus years of commutes and conference calls, your mind and body deserve a nice, long break. But after you've caught up on sleep, you can only rest for so long before your spirit starts pacing. Your human brain isn't wired for idleness. It craves engagement, challenge, curiosity, meaning. Without those elements, your days can start blending together, and that's when boredom, and sometimes even depression, can creep in.

I like to think of it this way: motion creates emotion. When you move physically, mentally, or creatively, you feel better. You think more clearly. You connect with people more deeply. That's why retired people who stay active—whether through volunteering or turning a hobby into a side gig—tend to be happier and healthier than those who just drift along. Data from a study called *Americans' Changing Lives* showed that retirees who volunteered had **higher well-being scores**, independent of other factors.

You don't need a packed schedule. You just need a few great reasons to get up in the morning.

I knew a surgeon who retired with great excitement. His first few months were wonderful. Golf three times a week, lunch with his buddies, plenty of naps. But as the novelty wore off, the sparkle dimmed. He started to feel invisible. His calendar was empty and his energy was depleted. No surgeries, hospital rounds, or seeing patients at the office. "I thought retirement would feel like freedom," he told me. "Instead, I'm just waiting to die." His experience hit me hard and vividly illustrated that without something engaging to move toward, your free time can become a looming void instead of an enticing gift.

The solution isn't to stay active for the sake of *busyness;* it's to stay engaged for the sake of *aliveness.* Rest refuels you for what's next, but that's only meaningful when what's next is something that matters to you. When you're passionate about what you do, whether that's collecting something, moderating a user group, or baking, rest becomes part of your fulfilling life's rhythm. You work, you play, you take a break and get refreshed, you start again.

So instead of asking yourself, "When do I get to stop?" ask, "What do I want to do and when do I want to start?" Which activities give you energy and which quietly drain it? Do you rest because you're fulfilled or because you're bored? What would make you look forward to tomorrow morning?

The goal isn't to replace your 9-to-5 routine with a grueling to-do list. You've proven that you can work hard; now it's about working joyfully. Your retirement days should look different and more balanced. For instance, you might spend your mornings working on creative projects, your afternoons going for walks and taking naps, and your evenings reading, listening to music, having a glass of wine with your family.

Passion is the best alarm clock

You know you've found the right retirement activities when you wake up excited and raring to go. Doing what you love doesn't have to involve changing the world; it just means you're still an active participant. Retirement is a chance to invest your time in what matters most to you. When you can embrace that mindset, you'll feel like "idle time" is overrated because you've discovered how much life you still have left to live.

PART II

The Paid Hobby Mindset

CHAPTER 5

The Joy of Doing What You'd Do for Free

THE FIRST TIME I GOT paid for doing a hobby I loved, it felt almost wrong, like I was getting away with something. I remember thinking, "Wait…they're paying me for this?" That's when it clicked: I wasn't working. I was doing what I'd gladly do for free, with a little income as the cherry on top. At the retirement stage of your life, you may be able to go off on new adventures will also earning a little money.

When people in the Baby Boomer generation were younger, work was a loaded word that signified pressure, performance, and office politics. Some of my elders would say "Quit complaining. Work is good for you." I wondered, "If work is so good for me, why do they have to pay me to do it?"

In retirement, you can choose projects that excite you, causes you're passionate about, and people you like to spend time with. You can say no without guilt and yes without fear of overcommitting. That's not like having a job; it's freedom with direction. And when you experience that magic, it's hard to imagine going back.

Joy first, income second

Being financially secure can change everything. When acquiring money stops being your motive, passion can take over as your guide. The richness of following your bliss can easily surpass the enjoyment of accumulating monetary wealth.

You can create art because you love the process. You can play music because you love the groove. You can consult because you like helping people overcome challenges. If a little income happens to accompany your favorite activities, great. If not, you're still doing something that brings you more alive.

It's funny how the universe rewards enthusiasm. When you do something with genuine joy, people notice. Your energy uplifts people. You get invited to play another gig, teach another class, join a community group. Before long, you realize you're again working, only on your terms. That's the magic of being retired with paid hobbies: you don't chase opportunities. They find you.

Here's the paradox: when you stop worrying about getting paid, you may end up earning more. Why? Because joy is palpable. People respond to authenticity. Whether they're wanting you to paint a commission piece or loving your improv, your enthusiasm draws people in. You're sharing your joy, and people are happy to pay for something that's made with passion. And the story doesn't end with income; in fact, that's where it gets more interesting. Because when you stop chasing a paycheck, you start noticing a different kind of wealth.

At this stage of life, being rich isn't about what's in your bank account. It's about what's in your day. Do you wake up ready to tackle something that excites you? Do you get to use your gifts, connect with others, and have a little fun along the way? Then congratulations, you're truly rich. The rest is just numbers.

Here's how I see it: passion + purpose + (optional) pay = fulfillment. When you spend your time doing what you'd do for free, every day feels like a small victory; a reminder that you've found your groove.

CHAPTER 6

Turn Passion into Purpose

CONFUCIUS SAID: "CHOOSE A JOB you love and you will never have to work a day in your life." That's only half true, because if you're not careful, you can turn what you love into just another job. Ask any hobbyist who accidentally built a business or any retiree who said yes to "just one more" consulting project that slowly monopolized their calendar. Passion can turn into pressure faster than you think. The trick is learning how to protect your joy while still giving your purpose room to grow.

It might begin innocently for you. Someone sees you doing something you're great at and remarks that "You should do this professionally."

At first, that's flattering. You start saying yes to opportunities, teaching a class, selling a cool thing you've invented. Then one day, you realize your to-do list is back, your calendar's full again, and you've somehow re-created the type of work environment you retired from.

That's when you have to hit the pause button and ask: Am I doing this because *I want to* or because I feel that I have to?

Passion vs. pressure

There's a fine line between purpose and pressure.

Passion energizes you.

Pressure drains you.

Passion makes you look forward to the day.

Pressure makes you check your watch.

In this chapter of life, your goal is to stay with the passion. If something you're doing starts feeling heavy, step back, reassess, simplify, or just say no. You don't owe anyone your time. You've paid those dues.

As your passion begins to take on a life of its own, staying grounded in the joy that sparked it will keep you feeling fulfilled. The antidote is simple: stay connected to why you're doing it. Playing music because it feeds your soul, not because you need the next booking. Teaching because you love seeing people eager to learn, not because you're chasing evaluations. Creating because it brings you joy, not because you're worried about likes, followers, or sales. If your why stays pure, your what will take care of itself.

Set boundaries to ensure that you don't lose your retirement "work-life balance." If you want to keep a hobby fun, treat your time as though it's precious (it is). Take breaks to rest and be open for spontaneity. Don't overcommit. You're retired, not on retainer. Saying no doesn't mean you're selfish; it means you're committed to protecting your time.

Here's one of the best parts of being retired with paid hobbies: you can quit anytime. If something stops being fun, you don't need to draft a resignation letter. You can just move on. That freedom changes the dynamic. You're no longer trapped by obligation. You're powered by enthusiasm. And oddly enough, that can make you even better at what you do because people can tell that you're doing it out of love, not duty.

Somewhere along the line, we were taught that expressing your purpose and play are opposites. They're not. In fact, the best kind of purpose feels like play. It's creative, energizing, and joy filled. When I'm teaching or performing, I'm in that zone where time disappears, energy flows, and I feel completely present. That's not work. That's living fully. That's where passion and purpose meet, in that sweet spot where "work" feels effortless.

So, here's the rule: if it starts to feel like work, take a break. If it feels like fun, keep going, but pace yourself. Because the whole point of retirement is to fill your remaining days with harmony and happiness.

When you become passionate about your purpose, you'll create a life that feels meaningful without heaviness. You don't have to chase achievement; you've already earned your stripes. Now it's about expression, contribution, and connection, the things that feed your spirit instead of embellish your résumé. You haven't retired from something. You've retired *to* something: activities that make you come alive.

CHAPTER 7

Think of Money as Gratitude

ONE OF THE FIRST QUESTIONS I hear when I tell people I'm retired with paid hobbies is, "So are you still working?"

The answer is no. "I'm retired—I just happen to earn money doing the things I love."

Their second question is: "Are you doing it for the money?"

Here's my answer: "Sometimes I get paid. Sometimes I don't. But that's not why I do it." Treating money as an expression of gratitude, not as your motivation for "working," is the mindset that makes all the difference in retirement.

What changes when income becomes optional instead of essential for you? How does it feel to be paid as an expression of appreciation rather than as an obligation?

When you were younger and working, money was probably the whole point. Every financial decision was driven by necessity and long-term security.

Now you've (we hope) done a good job of saving for this period of your life. The goal now isn't amassing wealth, it's reveling in meaning, connection, and a life you genuinely enjoy. That means that in retirement, a paycheck can become a trap. If you start chasing money, suddenly your hobby can feel like work. Deadlines creep in. Obligations pile up. Your pursuit turns into the type of activity you supposedly left behind.

Income as appreciation

The secret is to treat every dollar you earn as a thank-you gift, not a ticket you must punch to survive. Whether someone pays for a workshop you teach, a fan buys a ticket to your gig, or a neighbor hires you to help them build a deck, think "gratitude." Each payment is recognition that your time, skill, and creativity have value, and that's incredibly satisfying. Making money is optional; a bonus rather than a burden. You're not dependent on money, and that's liberating. You can do the project that excites you and skip the one that doesn't without worrying about paying the bills. When money isn't the driver, you can keep your activity fun and authentic.

Another advantage of treating money as a form of gratitude is that you can start measuring your success differently. It's not about how many pieces of furniture you can refinish or how many blog posts you can write. Ask yourself:

- Did I enjoy it?
- Did I feel like it was meaningful?
- Did my joyful actions bring joy to someone else?

If your answers are yes, it's easier to think of any income as icing on the cake.

Here's a funny thing: the moment you stop worrying about money, opportunities often multiply. People sense your authenticity. They feel your passion. They want to support you. The more you focus on realizing your talents and expressing your gifts, the more quickly income may naturally come to you. In other words, the better you get at doing what you love, the more the universe may reward you (and in cash).

Remember: the goal isn't to replace your career income. A few extra dollars here and there is nice for funding a new hobby, covering gear, or treating yourself or your friends to a nice meal. You're retired with paid hobbies, not working again. And if a little gratitude arrives in the form of a few greenbacks, that's just the universe applauding your spirit.

CHAPTER 8

Make Time Your New Currency

WHEN YOU RETIRE, YOU SUDDENLY have more of what everyone spends their lives chasing: time.

For decades, you may have felt like the clock was always against you, with meetings, deadlines, commutes, and obligations consuming your waking hours like a relentless tide. You were trading minutes for money, and every day seemed like a countdown.

Now? You're rich. Rich in hours and opportunities. How will you spend your precious remaining time on Earth?

Think of retirement as your new economy, one in which money is secondary and time is the main currency. Every hour you invest can yield fulfillment.

Unlike dollars, you can't earn more hours. Every minute of your life is finite, and the scarcity of time makes each moment priceless. How you spend them matters a lot.

While you were working to pay the bills, you may have invested time in things you didn't love to do. Now that you're retired, you can switch to doing only the things that light your fire, such as playing music that makes the audience get up and dance or coaching a kids' sports team. Each hour you spend in quality activity enriches your life. That freedom is liberating, but it also requires a new kind of discipline.

Budget time as you would money

In retirement, you can spend your hours on what you choose, without guilt or coercion. However, it's easy to fall into a hidden trap: distraction. Continual TV, endless inconsequential errands, hours scrolling social media, or overcommitting to projects that don't matter to you can quietly drain your time and energy. Remember, you can't get these precious hours back. Protect them as you would money in the bank. Yes, you can budget time just as carefully as you budget money. Spend it wisely. It's not about doing more; it's about doing what counts.

One way to do that is to be intentional about how you invest your time across four categories:

Essential time covers the non-negotiables; sleep, meals, and health routines that keep you functioning.

Meaningful time is work, service, or creative pursuits that give you purpose feeds your soul.

Joyful time is play: your hobbies, passions, and simple pleasures.

Social time nurtures your connections with family, friends, and community.

The trick is keeping the right balance of your time "currency." Overspend in one category and your investment in the others inevitably suffers. Ten hours of unpaid obligations, for example, may cost you ten hours in music, teaching, or time with people you love—a squandering of sorts that you'll never get back.

Here's another interesting difference in how you may feel about money in retirement. When you're working, one hour doing a stressful project may cost you more in happiness than any paycheck could ever make up for. In retirement, the value of time well spent may seem to exceed that of money. For instance, you might consider spending an hour of quality time with a friend or taking a pottery class to be priceless.

What's exciting about this new currency is choice. Do you want to:

Start a project?

Learn something new?

Travel, volunteer, or mentor?

Just sit and watch the sunset?

Every choice is an opportunity to invest in your own well-being. We call retirement "freedom" because you can spend your time on what truly matters to you.

The return on the time you invest in meaningful pursuits can be incredible. You can keep your skills sharp, your mind active. You can feel energized and happier by the day.

Unlike with money, you can't lose this type of contentment in a market crash. The more you invest in joy and purpose, spending your time wisely, the richer your life can become.

Here's a quick recap:

- Think of retirement as opening a new bank account, only instead of dollars, you're saving and spending hours.
- Invest those hours in doing things you love.
- Protect your precious remaining time from distractions.
- Let joy, purpose, and connection guide your hourly spending.

If you can do those things in retirement, you'll feel richer than you've ever felt in relation to your finances.

CHAPTER 9

The Seamstress Who Built a Business By Accident

WHEN SUE RETIRED FROM A career in medical technology, serving as a director of information systems, she swapped her lab equipment and computer for a sewing machine. Her plan was to sew for fun, make costumes and dresses and do alterations, and enjoy slow-paced mornings sipping coffee on her patio.

Then something unexpected happened. People started hearing about and seeing the products of Sue's sewing skills, and they were blown away.

"Those costumes are incredible! Do you sell them?"

"I'd love to buy some of your creations."

"Can you teach me how to sew like that?"

At first, Sue laughed it off. "No," she said. "I'm retired. I'm just doing this for fun."

But the requests kept coming. She realized people were willing to pay her for expressing her passion because they loved the manifestations of her creativity.

So she decided to cautiously experiment: a few alterations for neighbors. A bridesmaid dress for a friend. She didn't commit to doing it full time. She just let her passion naturally meet opportunity. Along with enjoying herself, she started generating income, and, over time, developed a small business that brought her lots of contentment without the trappings of "work."

Sue's sewing business is still hitting the sweet spot. She earns some income without losing freedom. She's in control through choosing when, how, and why to engage. Her story is a great example of what retirement can look like when you treat your passions as possibilities, not obligations.

As an unexpected bonus, she mentors to other retirees who want to sew, teach, or make their own creations. She shares her knowledge at workshops and encourages people to explore sewing without fear of failure. Her "accidental business" didn't just give her a little extra money, it gave her connection with new friends and a platform from which to inspire others.

As with Sue, retirement may surprise you. You'll start doing something small, simple, and fun, and people will notice. They'll admire your skills, be inspired by your proactiveness, and perhaps want to pay you for it. However, you don't need to chase money. You can follow your passion and let opportunities to earn a few bucks unfold. That's the essence of being retired with paid hobbies: fulfillment comes first and money may be the cherry on top.

CHAPTER 10

The Executive Who Made Gigs a Lifestyle

WHEN SAM RETIRED FROM A demanding career in healthcare, he went from being a part-time adjunct professor to a full-time lecturer. Unfortunately, that move turned out to be a disaster because of a department chair.

He'd also been an excellent guitar player and entertainer for more than 40 years, playing in clubs for fun. One evening shortly after he retired, he was asked to play in a fundraising event. He agreed, expecting a small, one-time performance. Instead, the room was packed, he got a standing ovation, and he received invitations to do more gigs.

With this experience Sam realized that music wasn't just a pastime for him, it could be a lifestyle he could build around in retirement. Local bar and restaurant owners wanted him on weekends. Community events needed performers. Friends and neighbors wanted him at their home concerts. He didn't need to go on tour; he could simply keep doing what he loved.

When fun gets noticed

Te key to Sam's making music a sustainable, energizing paid hobby was balance. He was selective, agreeing only to gigs that fit his schedule and energy. He was flexible, adjusting his performances around other commitments. He put fun first, never booking solely for money. If he wasn't going to enjoy it, he politely declined.

Like Sue, Sam also discovered an unexpected bonus. The gigs weren't just performances; they were opportunities to connect, collaborate, and create memories. He got to know old friends again and met new people who shared his musical interests.

The money came naturally as small fees, tips from appreciative audiences, and donations from special events. Sam focused on the music, and the universe made sure he was rewarded.

Then something else happened. Remember that he was dismayed by his experience as a lecturer? Through his relationship with me and my colleague, he was able to switch gears by picking up two adjunct professor positions.

That's the essence of the paid-hobby mindset: when you do what you love, the rest often takes care of itself. Joy can fuel your sustainability; you can continue for decades if you're having fun. Connecting with a community can enrich your social world. Optional income can keep you focused on your passion. Being flexible can preserve your freedom. Your enthusiasm can make people want to see, hear, and support you and your work.

Sam's story is another great example of how retirement can be a vibrant, deeply rewarding time. Whether it's art, teaching, or some other passion, the formula is the same:

- Follow what energizes you
- Share your gifts
- Protect your time for doing what you love
- Be open to earning a little money

Your retirement can be like a perfectly composed, meaningful song. You get to write the lyrics, set the rhythm, and play it at your own tempo.

The Concrete Worker Who Repurposed His Trade

FOR FORTY-FIVE YEARS, VINCE WORKED in concrete. The kind that sets hard, cracks knuckles, and holds buildings in place. He spent early mornings on construction jobs in steel-toed boots with weather that never seemed to cooperate, in a trade that left its mark on his body but made him proud. He stood up buildings, leveled sidewalks, and got jobs done. It was honest work, and Vince was very good at it. When people asked what he did for a living, his answer was "construction." End of story. Or so he thought.

Decades of skill building don't disappear

When Vince stepped away from his career, he didn't suddenly stop thinking in the languages of form, texture, and structure. Retirement didn't turn off that switch; it just changed the channel. What he stopped doing was chasing schedules, deadlines, and someone else's priorities. What he started doing, almost by accident, was letting his hands explore concrete differently.

Instead of slabs and footings, he began experimenting with shapes. Curves. Surfaces. Objects that didn't have to pass inspection or meet requirements on a spec sheet. He started creating concrete art and small sculptures, pieces that were tactile, expressive, and personal. This wasn't a business plan. It was curiosity.

To Vince, concrete had always been a material you control. You mix it right. You pour it right. You finish it right. But now he was discovering that it could also *respond*. Textures emerged. Shadows mattered. Imperfections became features instead of flaws.

Friends noticed. Then neighbors. Then someone said, "You should make one of those for me." Another asked if Vince could customize a piece. Another asked what he'd charge. Vince hadn't thought about charging; that wasn't the point. But when people started offering money for his art, something clicked. This wasn't just going to keep him busy. This was a chance to reframe a lifetime of skill.

What aligns Vince's story with a contented retirement so well is that money came second. There was no grand reinvention, no late-night panic about "What's next?"

Vince didn't brand himself as an artist overnight. He simply kept doing what felt right: small specialty projects, one-off pieces, custom work that blended art and functionality. Planters. Sculptural elements. Commissions no big contractor would have touched but that Vince could execute with ease. His clients weren't buying concrete. They were buying his forty-five years of expertise and his passion. Vince didn't retire *from* molding concrete; he simply started to use it on his own terms.

And then there was the music. Long before retirement, for fun, Vince had played keyboard in several bands. While concrete paid the bills, music fed his soul. He enjoyed rehearsals, gigs, and grooves that lived far away from job sites and hard hats.

After he retired from construction, I approached him about starting a large soul and rhythm and blues band. People thought we were nuts and it wouldn't go anywhere. But what started as my dream to get together with a few musician friends became Southtown Soul & Groove.

Now, Vince feels like his balance is just right. Concrete art satisfies the creator in him. Music satisfies his spirit. And both, unexpectedly, bring in a little money—just enough to make him feel valued.

Vince never set out to monetize his passion. He simply stayed open to what decades of knowledge could become when he was free from the grind. His story is confirmation that retirement isn't about stopping; it's about *redirecting*. The thing you did for a living could become the thing you do now for joy. The thing you do for joy now could become something people are happy to pay you for. And sometimes, the best opportunities show up when you're not chasing them.

CHAPTER 12

The Adjunct Professor Who Reinvented Himself

WHEN I RETIRED FROM FULL-TIME work, I faced a choice: slow down completely or stay engaged by teaching, playing music, and saying yes to new projects. I chose the latter, and that decision gave my days structure, kept my mind sharp, and filled my life with energy, connection, and purpose.

I didn't set out to get paid for my hobbies; it just kind of happened. One day, I connected with someone I'd known of in grad school but had never met. Maggie had left the grind of healthcare management and was teaching at Loyola University. They needed an adjunct professor at the School of Health Sciences and Public Health, and I'd spent twenty-five years as an adjunct professor at Governors State University and the University of Illinois, Chicago, teaching health care administration and quality. "Sure," I thought. "I love mentoring students, and I'd still have time for everything else I enjoy."

Then my band took off. We started playing at festivals, clubs, and summer concert series, all for the love of the music. Then the gigs started paying and the checks started coming in. That's when I realized that while I wasn't "working" anymore, I was doing what I loved, and the universe was rewarding me for it.

When Maggie asked if I'd consider teaching a course on healthcare administration, I jumped at the chance. I loved mentoring students. Part-time teaching wouldn't feel like work to me. I realized I still loved being in the classroom; the energy, the curiosity, the conversations. Even without the "full-time" title, I was a teacher at heart.

So, I turned the classroom into my retirement playground: a place to experiment, offer support, challenge students' ideas, and make myself useful again. Being an adjunct professor isn't glamorous and doesn't pay like a CEO job, but I wasn't doing it for the money. I was doing it because I wanted to enjoy helping students learn, think critically, and navigate the world of healthcare.

Part-time work in retirement has taught me that you don't have to quit contributing. I set my own schedule. I pick my projects. I get to teach in a way that feels authentic. My students get an engaged, experienced teacher, and I get to do something I love without the stress of a full-time obligation. That's a win-win. It bolsters the philosophy that retirement isn't about stopping work; it's about choosing work that energizes you.

Teaching and playing feed each other

Around the same time, my band started picking up more gigs. I'd always been passionate about playing music. I worked as a musician in the '70s and then continued for fun. Now, performing was becoming a chance to express myself, connect with people, and earn a little money.

Together, these two activities became my ticket to a rewarding retirement.

I also realized that there are parallels between teaching and performing: both are about connection. Both are about presence. Both are about giving something meaningful to others. Teaching pays me in knowledge and inspiration. Music pays me in energy, smiles, and a powerful sense of togetherness.

They also feed each other. Teaching keeps my mind sharp, which makes my music performances more focused and energetic. Playing music keeps me creative, which makes my classroom presentation more engaging. Both bring me unexpected opportunities; workshops, festivals, speaking engagements.

And that's the part most people miss. This turn of events didn't happen by accident, and it isn't unique to me. It's the result of making a few intentional choices about how to use your time, talent, and curiosity in retirement.

When you can see how those pieces fit together, you realize that this kind of life isn't just possible, it's repeatable.

What I learned is when you pursue what you love in retirement, everything else can fall into place. You're not stuck between leisure and work; you're thriving in a space where passion, purpose, and practicality intersect, and your life feels richer for it.

Find Your People Network

RETIREMENT CAN FEEL LIKE YOU'RE stepping off of a moving walkway. Everyone is still whizzing by, but you're suddenly walking at a relaxed pace. Freedom from work is wonderful in theory, but in reality, it can make you feel a bit lonely and isolated in your hobbies. After all, humans are social creatures. Even in retirement, we need connection with others.

That's where a people network comes in. This isn't just your friends, but it's also not about having dozens of contacts on LinkedIn. It's about depth. You want people who understand your passions, share your interests, and support your journey.

Find people who inspire you, challenge you, and can celebrate your successes without jealousy. Those are the ones who can form the foundation of a rich, meaningful retirement. Your network might include:

- Gardeners who swap tips and cuttings
- Authors who meet to critique and inspire each other
- Students, mentees, or colleagues who value your guidance

Your people can:
- Offer encouragement when you try something new
- Provide feedback to help you grow
- Celebrate your successes with you
- Share opportunities you might overlook

You don't have to find your people all at once. Start small. Attend a workshop. Join a club. Go to a performance or class. New relationships can deepen over time, creating a network that's a cornerstone of your retirement life.

Here's the beauty of having a supportive group: your people can help make you accountable without pressure. For instance, you'll be more likely to show up for a volunteer event if others are counting on you. You can share ideas and encouragement with your network to help keep your passion alive, as well as be inspired by what others are doing.

In addition, you may stumble on unexpected opportunities through interacting with your people. Your network can amplify what you love, perhaps in ways you never imagined. For instance, maybe you share a hobby story at a community event and weeks later receive an email asking you to **consult, mentor, or guest teach**—something you never thought of doing as a "service." Your network can be an incubator for new opportunities, collaborations, and paid hobbies. For example, a neighbor might ask your band to play at a fundraiser, a friend might invite you to display your art at a local farmer's market, or someone in your chess club might ask you for advice, which could lead to your giving a workshop.

There's something magical about sharing an experience with people who "get it" along with you, such as when you're planning a river cleanup or swapping gardening triumphs and failures. Shared joy can turn ordinary activities into memorable experiences. Finding your people can transform your retirement from a solitary journey into a social adventure. You're still free, flexible, and pursuing your passions, but now you can do it alongside other people who naturally understand you and bond with you over your mutual passions.

Retirement doesn't need to be a solo act. When you find your people, it can be a veritable symphony.

CHAPTER 14

Fail Forward

IN YOUR CAREER, MISTAKES HAD consequences: lost opportunities, missed promotions, an awkward conversation with the boss. In retirement? Not so much. Risk-taking now looks different because:

- You're financially secure enough to try something just for fun
- You can say yes or no without fear of losing your bonus
- You can walk away if you stop enjoying it

This freedom changes the equation, allowing you to pursue projects with curiosity instead of anxiety. If you fail, it can be a less catastrophic experience—a "teaching moment"—maybe even a source of laughter and joy.

The key to thriving with paid hobbies in retirement is embracing the mindset of learning, adjusting, and advancing *because of* the failure.

- A garden that didn't thrive can teach you what would work next season
- A painting that didn't sell can teach you what might resonate better with your fans

- A gig that flopped can teach you how to connect better with the audience

It's OK if some of your attempts fail. Some may surprise you. Each "failure" is a chance to gather feedback, adjust, and a step toward doing what brings you fulfillment.

Paid hobbies are perfect for experimentation because the stakes are low and the rewards can be high. For instance, you can:

- Try a new instrument, a different genre, or getting a new bandmate
- Offer a workshop on a topic you've never taught
- Do a small creative project without a formal business plan

The more you experiment, the more likely you'll be to discover new joys, skills, and opportunities. Here are some examples:

The musician who tried a new gig: The first performance at a local festival didn't go well, but trying again with a different setlist led to recurring bookings and a loyal audience.

The artist who experimented: After another brushstroke, a painting style that initially sold poorly became her signature style.

The seamstress who expanded: A first workshop was chaotic, but through small tweaks, she transformed it into a sought-after community event.

In each of these situations, failure wasn't an end point, it was a stepping stone.

The golden rule of retirement experimentation is "Fun first." Failing is easier when you're not under pressure. If you fail and you're not enjoying what you're doing, stop and consider why you're doing it or how you could enjoy it more. If you fail while you're enjoying yourself, is there still a way to improve your approach?

Thriving retirees share three key attitudes:

- They're more curious than cautious, trying things they've wondered about
- They're more joyful than judgmental, focusing on the process, not on comparing themselves to others
- They're open to learning as opposed to seeking perfection, treating mistakes as lessons instead of liabilities

Adopting these attitudes can help you turn your retirement from a slow wind-down into an enticing adventure.

Experiment boldly. Learn continually. Laugh about your mistakes. Aim for having more fun.

When failure constitutes helpful feedback, every hobby or project becomes an opportunity to grow, connect, and enjoy your life more fully. In retirement, failure can be just another ride that can make your journey richer.

Design the Retirement of Your Dreams

RETIREMENT ISN'T ABOUT SLOWING DOWN; it's about designing the life you want in your older years. After decades of adhering to schedules, meeting deadlines, and satisfying obligations, you have the freedom to choose exactly how you want to spend your days. This is your chance to intentionally create a life that reflects who you are and what you love.

As you've learned, the foundation of a well-designed retirement is passion. What makes your heart race with excitement? What activities make you lose track of time? What talents do you want to explore further?

Your passions aren't just hobbies, they are the raw materials for a life that feels meaningful.

Next, layer in purpose. Purpose turns joy into contribution. What you enjoy doing begins to matter beyond yourself when it's shared—teaching students, mentoring colleagues, or volunteering your experience where it's needed. It might mean offering your music, art, or writing to others, not for applause or income but for connection. It can be as simple as using your skills to help your community thrive.

Purpose gives your time depth. It ensures that your paid hobbies are more than just fun; they become meaningful, outward-facing expressions of who you are and what you value.

Think of this as a design problem, not a financial one. The formula is simple: passion + purpose + optional income = fulfillment. Paid hobbies aren't meant to replicate a former paycheck; they're design elements that enrich your life with joy, meaning, and momentum. Income becomes a bonus—feedback that what you're creating resonates—along with a resource that funds further exploration. In this design, flexibility and enjoyment come first. Time is your new currency. Spend it intentionally. Remember, the goal isn't to fill every hour but to fill your life with meaning.

- Prioritize activities that energize and inspire you.
- Protect your schedule from stress and distraction.
- Build routines that balance fun, learning, connection, and rest.
- Surround yourself with like-minded people.
- Collaborate with and support your "colleagues."
- Celebrate your successes, learn from your failures, and keep moving forward.

A strong network of people can amplify your joy, open doors, and keep your retirement vibrant. Designing your life now encompasses an ongoing process of trying new hobbies, experimenting with paid projects, failing forward and adjusting, and keeping fun at the center so that flexibility and curiosity allow you to evolve with your interests. Freedom remains your ultimate gift: the ability to choose how you live, pursue joy without guilt, share your gifts on your terms, and align your passion, purpose, people, and time in days that are fully lived.

Designing your retirement life is a bit like creating a masterpiece:

- Your passions give your life color.

- Your purpose gives it depth by connecting what you enjoy to what matters.
- Paid hobbies add sparkle by introducing validation, momentum, and surprise—someone values what you love enough to support it.
- Time and people provide the frame.

You're no longer following someone else's plan. You're crafting a life that's meaningful, joyful, and uniquely yours. Retirement is your opportunity to do what you love, share your gifts with others, and occasionally get paid along the way.

CHAPTER 16

Create A Retirement Blueprint

GREAT! YOU'VE READ STORIES, WISDOM, and rules about retiring with paid hobbies, and I hope you're starting to get inspired to apply these principles. Now it's time to create a plan for putting this approach into practice.

Step 1: Identify your passions

Deci & Ryan's Self-Determination Theory (1991, 1995) explains that intrinsic motivation, behavior driven by internal satisfaction rather than external rewards, is powered by three psychological needs: autonomy, competence (mastery), and relatedness (connection). When these needs are met, people experience deeper engagement and passion for activities.

One model built on this theory is Robert J. Vallerand's Dualistic Model of Passion, which defines passion as "a strong inclination toward a self-defining activity that one loves, values, and invests time and energy in on a regular basis." This model shows that passion arises when people internalize activities into their identity and value them personally, not just for external rewards.

With that in mind, you can start by making a list of what excites and energizes you: Hobbies you love. Skills you want to develop. Activities in which you lose track of time. Circle the ones that feel most essential.

Step 2: Identify your purpose

Ask yourself: how can my passions serve others?

Can you teach, mentor, or lead workshops? Can you share your art, music, or creations with a wider audience? Can you contribute to your community or help promote causes you care about? Purpose isn't a single destination or universal calling. As author Viktor Frankl noted "in the book *Man's Search for Meaning*", meaning is personal and situational. For some people, it shows up through service or teaching; for others, through expression, craftsmanship, or creating beauty.

Step 3: Map your time

Time is your most valuable asset. You get to decide what deserves it. When you map your time, you may discover you spend hours maintaining habits that no longer serve you—and minutes on the things you say matter most. The map gives you permission to rebalance.

Daily routines: Balance energy, rest, and joy.

Weekly schedule: Allocate time for hobbies, social connections, and new experiments.

Flex days: Allow room for spontaneity, discovery, and exploration.

Step 4: Build your people network

Your people network is more than a list of contacts. It's a source of accountability, joy, and new opportunities. By engaging with groups, clubs, hobby communities, mentors, students, and collaborators, you can surround yourself with people who share your passions, will encourage you to follow through, and can open doors you might never find alone. Building a network means following your curiosity, showing up consistently, contributing generously, and nurturing your relationships. Over time, these connections can deepen your experiences, inspire you, and expand your life in ways that enrich both your pursuits and your day-to-day routines.

Step 5: Plan for experimentation

Give yourself space to experiment and explore. Take on a short-term project such as hosting a one-time workshop, starting a small artwork or music series, or teaching a mini-class to see how your ideas land. Try a new creative direction in your hobby: write a song in a style you've never tackled, cook something from a new type of cuisine, or paint a subject you've avoided. To test your skills and interests, you can accept occasional paid opportunities, such as a one-off commission, gig, or consulting session, in a low-pressure way. Treat missteps not as failures but as feedback. Each attempt can teach you what resonates, what energizes you, and where your passion is strongest.

Step 6: Check for fun

Ask yourself, "Does this activity feel energizing?" Prioritize what excites and inspires you. Remove or adjust how you approach any activities that feel like drudgery.

C H A P T E R   1 7 :

Plan Your First Three Months

RETIREMENT IS LIKE OPENING A brand-new notebook. The first pages you write set the tone for everything that follows. The first ninety days after you stop working are key, as they can help you create momentum, confidence, and clarity about what your new life will look like.

Your early months of retirement shouldn't be about getting it right but about getting started. Reflection, experimentation, making meaningful connections with people, and using your time well can create strong momentum. When you approach retirement with curiosity, you can make it more than a break from work. It becomes a playground for creativity, connection, and fulfillment.

Here's some guidance to get you started.

Note: Using a designated retirement-planning notebook can help you keep track of your progress.

Weeks 1–2: Reflect and prioritize

Goal: Identify 3–4 activities to focus on.

Write down all the activities you've loved, hobbies you've neglected, and skills you want to explore. Assess your passion levels and whether any of your activities could also benefit others. Define your "fun metric": what makes you feel joyful in an activity rather than like you're working?

Weeks 3–4: Explore and experiment

Goal: Gain firsthand experience about what energizes you most.

Choose one or two hobbies to experiment with. Attend a class, workshop, or local event to gauge your interest. Try a small paid opportunity if available, like selling one or two pieces of artwork, but remember, money is optional.

Weeks 5–6: Start building your network

Goal: Establish connections with people who inspire and motivate you.

Engage with groups, clubs, hobby communities, mentors, students, and collaborators. Show up consistently, contribute generously, and follow your curiosity.

Weeks 7–8: Plan your time

Goal: Create a weekly schedule that balances meaningful work, creative play, rest, and connection. Leave some downtime for spontaneous opportunities and unexpected inspiration. You want to balance your time spent on:

- Hobbies
- Social engagements
- Learning and personal growth
- Rest and reflection

Week 9–10: Explore optional income

Goal: Test how income could fit naturally into your retired life without making you feel stressed.

Identify one opportunity to earn a little money, for example, a workshop you could teach or something you could make and sell. Treat it as a learning experience and assess how it went. Did you love doing it? Could you do more? Should you adjust?

Weeks 11–12: Reflect, edit, and celebrate

Goal: Finish your first three months with clarity, confidence, and a sense of purpose.

- Review: In your notebook, take stock of what brought you the most fulfillment.
- Adjust: Drop what isn't working and expand what is.
- Applaud: Note your achievements, skills you've learned, people you've met, and other wins.

CHAPTER 18

Keep Your Spark Alive

RETIREMENT IS IDEALLY A MARATHON, not a sprint. Your first 90 days may be exciting, but maintaining your energy through the years may require some effort. This chapter is about helping you keep your spark alive so you can continue to feel vibrant and energized.

Curiosity is the engine of long-term engagement. It can keep your mind sharp, your passions fresh, and your enthusiasm high. You can stay curious by:

- Exploring new techniques, styles, and approaches in your hobbies
- Expanding your knowledge by attending workshops, lectures, and other events
- Experimenting with new pursuits such as learning a second language, playing a musical instrument, or doing a creative writing project

What (still) makes you curious? What do you want to learn next? Periodically revisit your retirement blueprint. What's working? What's not? Adjust your time allocations to match your energy levels and interests. Reassess whom you want to keep spending time with.

When you allow your retirement activities to evolve, they can grow with you instead of settling you into stagnation. Successful long-term engagement with like-minded people can help you maintain enthusiasm, accountability, and fun. That means:

- Keep nurturing your relationships with friends, collaborators, and mentors
- Introduce yourself to new people who bring fresh ideas or energy
- Celebrate your and your friends' successes and support each other through setbacks

Balance exertion and rest

Even in retirement, you can get burned out on what you're doing. Long-term fulfillment in this phase of your life comes from sustainability, not constant hustle. You can pace yourself by:

- Respecting your limits (knowing how much time, energy, and commitment you can give **without turning enjoyment into obligation)**
- Scheduling time for rest and reflection
- Rotating activities to prevent fatigue in any one pursuit
- Taking small, low-pressure risks

Whether you've finished a successful performance, grown a thriving garden, or had a piece of art shown in a local gallery, you can enliven your spark by taking time to celebrate it. Recognition, including self-recognition, fuels ongoing engagement.

- Reflect on your progress
- Share your achievements with some people in your network

- Use achieving success as an opportunity to continue exploring and discovering, not as an endpoint. Keep your focus on what you're enjoying, not on the output.

Keeping your spark alive in retirement is about curiosity, connection, balance, and celebration. By staying curious, nurturing your people network, respecting your energy, experimenting creatively, and celebrating your progress, you can ensure that your next decade (and beyond?) is vibrant and fully aligned with your passions.

CHAPTER 19

Create Your Retirement Legacy

RETIREMENT IS MORE THAN A stage of life that can be supremely rewarding; it's an opportunity to leave a lasting mark. You're purposefully pursuing your hobbies can leave ripples far beyond your experience. The greatest legacy of retiring with paid hobbies isn't the money you earn or the accolades you receive. Legacy is about what you plant, nurture, and share, not how much money you make. When you retire with paid hobbies, in addition to enjoying freedom, you can make a lasting impression on your family (even on future generations), friends, community members, and other people. That's because your hobbies and passions can carry your life story forward.

Your music can create memorable moments for those in attendance. Your artwork and writing can inspire others to be creative. Volunteering at venues such as a gardening club can strengthen the human ties in your local community. By pursuing your passions, you can inspire people around you to pursue theirs.

The relationships you cultivate can also be part of your legacy. Mentoring younger colleagues or students transfers knowledge and wisdom to them. Collaborating with peers can strengthen your community and social bonds by creating shared experiences, building trust, and giving everyone a chance to contribute, learn, and enjoy the process together. Sharing your experiences can encourages others to be curious and embrace their own growth.

Your people network can be a testament to the impact of your engagement in the world. Through pursuing your hobbies, you can model that:

- When you know your purpose, you can channel that energy into activities that bring you joy.
- Curiosity can fuel lifelong growth.
- Taking risks and occasionally failing is healthy.
- Having fun is a metric of fulfillment.

By pursuing your passions, you can help create opportunities for:
- Students, who may be inspired to pursue careers or take on projects they hadn't considered
- Fellow hobbyists, who may feel encouraged to develop their own skills
- Community members, who may feel inspired by your volunteer work

Even seemingly small actions can matter:
- A workshop you give could ignite a lifelong passion in an attendee
- A planted garden can feed neighbors and brighten a community space
- A book you write can empower people to take action
- A performance can lift people's spirits, strengthen bonds, and create wonderful memories for people

The
Retired With Paid Hobbies
Cheat Sheet

1. **Lead with passion.** If it's not fun, don't do it.
2. **Express your purpose.** Do what you love in ways that help or inspire others.
3. **Treat money as gratitude.** Income can take the form of appreciation, not compensation.
4. **Protect your time,** your valuable limited resource.
5. **Find your people.** Grow your joy faster in a community.
6. **Experiment freely.** Use failure as feedback, not defeat.
7. **Prioritize fun.** If it feels heavy, adjust.

Enjoy Your Journey

CONGRATULATIONS! YOU'VE FINISHED THIS BOOK, and now it's time to turn your post-work life into a vibrant, playful, and purposeful experience. Think of your retirement years as a blank canvas waiting for your unique brushstrokes. Your hobbies—paid or not—are perfect venues for expressing your passions and enjoying all the attending benefits.

So, what are you waiting for? Go ahead, retire in a fantastic way. Pick up that musical instrument. Enroll in that course. Join that local hiking group. Experiment, enjoy, fail, if necessary, adjust, and move forward. The world is waiting for your unique combination of interests and experience. Get started today!

About the Author

GEORGE EINHORN IS A SEMI-RETIRED educator, speaker, and adjunct professor at Loyola University Chicago, where he continues to teach and mentor students after a long career in leadership and education. Blending academic insight with real-world experience, George has become a trusted voice on navigating life's next chapter with intention and curiosity.

Outside the classroom, George leads *Southtown Soul & Groove*, a successful Soul and R&B tribute band. What began as a passion project evolved into a profitable and deeply fulfilling endeavor—offering living proof that "paid hobbies" can enhance both income and quality of life in retirement.

Through speaking, teaching, and writing, George helps retirees and near-retirees rethink traditional notions of retirement. His work focuses on turning personal interests into purpose-driven income, strengthening identity beyond a former career, and designing a retirement that balances meaning, creativity, and joy.

For more information, email the author at:
geinhorn1953@gmail.com.